THE EXTRAORDINARY LIFE OF

SERENA
WILLIAMS

THE EXTRAORDINARY LIFE OF
SERENA
WILLIAMS

Written by Shelina Janmohamed
Illustrated by Ashley Evans

Kane Miller
A DIVISION OF EDC PUBLISHING

WHO IS
Serena
Williams?

Serena Jameka Williams

is one of the most successful *tennis champions* ever.
She has played professionally for nearly twenty-five
years and she has been the *world number one* eight
times. Many people consider her the greatest female
tennis player of all time. She is also a businesswoman,
an actor and a fashion icon. She has set up her own
charity, which helps poor children across the world.
And she is a mother.

When she was a child Serena *dreamed* of being the best tennis player in the world. She knew that to make her dreams come true she would have to **work hard.** She faced many challenges along the way. Her family wasn't rich enough to pay for tennis lessons or coaches, which can be very expensive; they didn't even know anyone who played tennis!

Her father got the idea when he was watching tennis on TV, then he studied the sport and started *coaching* his children himself. Serena had to practice on tennis courts in dangerous areas, using poor-quality rackets and balls that were worn out.

Some prejudiced people told Serena that she shouldn't be a tennis champion because of the color of her skin; others CRITICIZED the way she looked. Sometimes her poor health nearly stopped her; her knees and her foot have needed surgery, and she almost died from complications after the birth of her daughter. Serena refused to let these setbacks stop her.

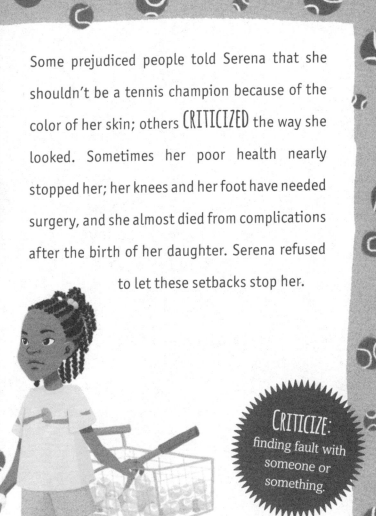

CRITICIZE: finding fault with someone or something.

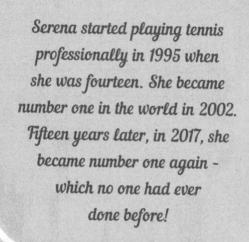

Serena started playing tennis professionally in 1995 when she was fourteen. She became number one in the world in 2002. Fifteen years later, in 2017, she became number one again - which no one had ever done before!

Like many champions, she lost some matches, but that just made her even more determined to win again.

Her older sister Venus is also a tennis champion. Sometimes they compete against each other, and sometimes they play together in **doubles matches**. It's important to Serena that they support each other and remain strong as sisters.

So, what is the secret of her success?

"YOU HAVE TO *believe in yourself,* WHEN NO ONE ELSE DOES."

It all started when she was just three years old and picked up a tennis racket.

"IT DOESN'T MATTER WHAT *your background is* OR WHERE YOU COME FROM, IF YOU HAVE *dreams and goals,* THAT'S ALL THAT MATTERS."

Early life

Serena was born on September 26, 1981, in Saginaw, Michigan. Her father, Richard Williams, ran a security firm. Her mother, Oracene "Brandy" Price, was a nurse. Serena had *four older sisters*: Yetunde, Lyndrea, Isha and Venus.

Serena's father had big plans for the five girls. One day after watching tennis on TV he told Serena's mom that he thought their children should become **tennis champions**. He started studying the game by reading books and watching videos, taught himself and Oracene to play, and then they started coaching their daughters. He even wrote a seventy-eight-page plan of how Serena and Venus were going to become tennis world champions!

The whole family moved to Compton in California when Serena was just a few months old. It was a very poor and often dangerous neighborhood. Richard thought it would toughen up the girls – he believed that **hard work** and having a **strong character** were essential if they were to succeed in life.

The seven members of the Williams family lived in a small white house with two bedrooms. A chain-link fence and an old tree were in the front, and at the back was a tiny yard. The five sisters *shared one room* with two bunk beds. As the youngest, Serena snuggled in with whomever she felt like at nighttime. They were a very close, *loving family*.

As a child Serena was mischievous, fearless and very **competitive**. When the family put on talent shows with each other for fun, Serena always made sure she won.

Serena was close to all her sisters, but everyone knew that she wanted to grow up to be like *Venus*. Serena looked up to her big sister, who took care of her. Venus would use her pocket money to buy treats for her little sister.

Serena learned to work hard from a very young age. She was just *two years old* when she started accompanying her dad to deliver phone books.

Serena the tennis player

Every day the parents and five daughters would wake up at 6 a.m. and head to their local **tennis courts** for practice. Sometimes the family climbed into their faded-yellow VW van and headed to courts farther away. One of the car seats had been removed so there was space for a supermarket cart full of worn-out tennis balls.

Before they could play, Richard had to sweep the courts clean of broken glass. He jokingly called the tennis courts the "Compton Hills Country Club" to make them sound grand. His *imagination and humor* transformed the courts into something magical, a place where anything was possible.

As a toddler Serena sat in her stroller while she watched her sisters play. When she was three years old she stood on the court with a racket for the *first time*.

She wasn't to know then that seventeen years later, at the age of twenty, she would be standing on a tennis court at WIMBLEDON, having just become the world's number one female tennis player.

WIMBLEDON

in London is the home of The Championships, Wimbledon – the oldest tennis tournament in the world.

"I LEARNED
HOW IMPORTANT IT IS
to fight for a dream
AND, MOST IMPORTANTLY, TO

DREAM BIG.

MY FIGHT BEGAN WHEN
I was three
AND I HAVEN'T
TAKEN A BREAK SINCE."

The family practiced **before and after** school. To build their stamina they had to run drills up and down the court.

Venus would play against their dad, and Serena would play against their mom. Practicing every day was tough, and sometimes Serena would be envious of her friends, who got to hang out together after school.

But she realized as she grew up that this gave her an **advantage** over other tennis players.

Serena and Venus didn't wear professional tennis clothes, but would dress in **jeans** to play.

"I want tacos.

EVERY DAY I WANT TACOS.

I DON'T KNOW WHAT TO DO?

IS THERE HELP FOR SOMEONE THAT WANTS TO

EAT TACOS

every day?"

Sometimes the courts were a dangerous place. One day a car drove by and a man on the roof started shooting a gun. The girls threw themselves onto the ground to stay safe. Whenever they heard gunfire they would keep down until the danger had passed. Although it was *frightening*, it focused Serena's mind.

"*If you can keep playing tennis* WHEN SOMEONE IS *shooting a gun* DOWN THE STREET, THAT'S CONCENTRATION!"

A champion in the making

Serena entered her first **tennis tournament** when she was just four and a half. Over the next five years she won forty-six out of forty-nine tournaments, and eventually she was listed as **number one** in the under-tens.

In 1991, when Serena was ten years old, Richard and Oracene felt that Venus and Serena needed a **professional coach** to take their game to the next level. The girls had already made a name for themselves in California. Richard took a chance and called **Rick Macci**, who ran a tennis academy in Florida. Richard persuaded him to fly to Compton to see Venus and Serena in action.

"**WHAT BLEW ME AWAY WAS THEIR**

burning desire

TO RUN AND FIGHT AND

GET TO EVERY BALL LIKE

their hair was on fire.

I HAD NEVER SEEN TWO KIDS

TRY SO HARD.

I HAD NEVER SEEN BODIES

THAT COULD MOVE LIKE THAT."

– Rick Macci

Rick had already coached many successful tennis champions, but he saw something really special in the talent and determination of the two sisters, and he invited them to become students at his school. This was an *incredible opportunity* for the girls to receive the world-class coaching they needed to compete at a professional level. But the Williams family simply didn't have the money to pay for the move.

Yet again, Richard Williams took a chance. He found SPONSORSHIP DEALS for his daughters. With that money they moved to *Florida* and bought a home near the tennis academy. It was the next chapter in Serena's journey to becoming a champion.

SPONSORSHIP: when a company or individual pays someone to advertise their product.

Doing things differently

The family lived in Delray Beach, north of Fort Lauderdale, in Florida. At ten and eleven, Serena and Venus were enrolled in a local school. Every day after school Richard drove them to the academy for tennis practice. They played *six hours a day, six days a week, for four years*.

Richard and Oracene felt this was a lot for the girls, so they decided to homeschool them so they could focus better on their tennis and their studies. Education always came first. If their grades were dropping, their parents would cut back on tennis practice.

Their practice time was carefully monitored so that they didn't injure themselves. They were also encouraged to have **_interests beyond tennis_**, and they tried out other activities like guitar playing, roller-skating, surfing and reading. Serena started to develop many different talents.

DID YOU KNOW?

Serena's favorite food is her mom's chicken with rice and gravy, which she's loved since she was a child.

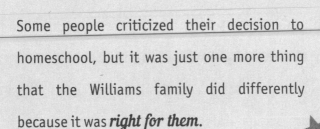

Some people criticized their decision to homeschool, but it was just one more thing that the Williams family did differently because it was *right for them*.

Then Richard did yet another very surprising thing: he stopped entering Venus and Serena into junior tournaments. Richard didn't want his daughters to learn the same techniques as everyone else – he wanted them to stand out.

Usually people become tennis champions by competing as a junior first.

"WE DO OUR **OWN** THING . . . .

WE'RE VERY

different

FROM EVERYONE ELSE,

BECAUSE WE

think differently."

– Venus Williams

By avoiding competitions the girls would also **save time** by not traveling, and could instead focus on their studies. There was one more very serious reason why Richard didn't want Venus and Serena to compete – he was worried about the racism the girls might experience.

When Serena was growing up it was rare to see high-profile black players in tennis. Even though tennis has been played in the US since 1874, it was only in 1950 that black people were allowed to participate in the US Nationals. The first black player was Althea Gibson. In 1957 she became the first black American to win a Grand Slam title at the US Open. In fact, the next black woman to win a Grand Slam singles title would be Serena in 1999.

ALTHEA GIBSON 1957

SERENA WILLIAMS 1999

Sadly Richard and Oracene had found that some white parents at the tournaments would speak in insulting ways about Serena and Venus because they were black. It wasn't something that they wanted their daughters to endure, so to **protect them** they stopped them from taking part.

Four years later, in 1995, the girls started competing again. That same year, Serena and Venus left Rick Macci's academy. It was also the year that Serena turned professional. She was just

fourteen years old.

The rise and rise
of Serena Williams

Serena's DEBUT as a tennis professional was very shaky. In fact, she wasn't even supposed to play as a pro because the minimum age was sixteen. But Serena found a way around the rules by securing a wild-card entry. She lost in the first round.

DEBUT:
first appearance or performance.

Serena decided to take a year off from competitions. During this time she was busy with her high school studies. No longer homeschooled, she now went to a small school and loved being an ordinary student like everyone else.

DID YOU KNOW?

Serena's classmates sometimes described her as the class clown because she was such fun.

She also continued to work hard at her tennis. When she was practicing tennis at home her father put huge placards in their front yard to **motivate** her and Venus. In capital letters they read:

SERENA,
YOU MUST
LEARN
TO LISTEN

and

VENUS, WHEN
YOU FAIL
YOU FAIL
ALONE.

Serena played her next professional match in 1997 at the age of fifteen, but despite losing three more events, she did not give up on her dream. Instead she became even more **determined** to succeed.

The top 100

Eventually Serena started to win some important matches, including beating two top-ten players.

This catapulted her into the world's top-100 female tennis players in 1997. It was hard work, but Serena kept going. She still lost matches, but that didn't stop her from getting up after each defeat, learning from her mistakes and *trying harder*.

"I REALLY THINK

A CHAMPION

IS DEFINED NOT BY THEIR

wins

BUT BY HOW THEY CAN

RECOVER WHEN THEY

fall."

Her determination paid off and in July 1998 she had her first huge victory: winning a GRAND SLAM at Wimbledon in the mixed doubles with Belarusian player *Max Mirnyi*. She made an impression on the audience, braiding white beads into her hair that made a noise every time she took a step.

GRAND SLAM:
the name for the four most important annual tennis events – the Australian Open, the French Open, Wimbledon and the US Open.

Serena was just sixteen and this was only the beginning, so she kept playing hard, winning some matches and losing others. The key was to *keep going*, keep improving and to become the best.

Max Mirnyi said Serena was "fierce" and had a "warrior spirit."

Sisterhood

During this period Serena's *biggest rival* on the court was Venus. They often found themselves playing each other in the finals of singles competitions. But they weren't just competitors; sometimes they were partners fighting for victory in the *women's doubles*. They were best friends and extremely close sisters, but as soon as they were playing tennis Serena became fiercely *competitive*. However, she knew that whatever happened on the court, whether she won or lost, at the end of the day she would still be Venus's sister and that was the most important thing.

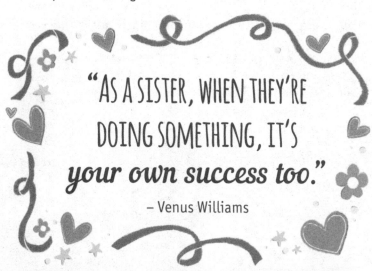

"AS A SISTER, WHEN THEY'RE DOING SOMETHING, IT'S *your own success too.*"

– Venus Williams

Venus and Serena have competed against each other in thirty matches. They have won twenty-two titles when they've played together.

In tennis, two people are positioned on opposite sides of the court, divided by a net. They hit a ball back and forth over the net. The ball must land in the opponent's court so that they cannot return it over the net. A player that achieves this wins a point.

A player must win at least four points to win a game, and at least six games to win a set. To win a match a player must achieve either two out of three sets, or three out of five sets. When the match is played one-on-one it is called "singles." Matches can also be played in pairs, which is called "doubles."

"THERE IS NO WAY I WOULD BE AT [NUMBER] ONE **WITHOUT HER.** *She is my inspiration.* SHE IS THE ONLY REASON I AM STANDING HERE TODAY."

In early matches Venus always won, but as Serena grew in *experience and confidence* she started to beat her sister. In September 1999, Serena won her first singles Grand Slam title at the US Open, beating the number one player at the time, Martina Hingis! She was now officially one of the world's

top-ten
female tennis
players.

Olympic champions

Venus and Serena played
together at the Olympics in Sydney
in 2000 and won a gold medal in
the women's doubles. They were
now Olympic champions.

While Serena was playing in *international tournaments* she also made sure to focus on her studies. It was a lot to balance. She had to miss her **high school prom** because she was at the French Open! In the summer of 1999 her hard work paid off and she *graduated* from high school.

Standing up and standing out

When she was seventeen years old Serena's parents gave her an important piece of advice:

"BE HAPPY AND BE *yourself.*"

She has had to remember this during her life, especially in the coming years when she faced criticism that was often unfair.

Serena was always herself. She played in a **unique style.** She dressed on the court with hair and clothes that she chose. She was a strong, talented, determined, passionate young black woman.

"I FEEL LIKE I DEFINITELY WAS
SCRUTINIZED BECAUSE I WAS CONFIDENT –

I WAS BLACK AND

I was confident.

AND I AM BLACK

AND I AM CONFIDENT.

BUT I WOULD SAY, 'I FEEL LIKE I CAN BE

NUMBER ONE.'

WELL, WHY SHOULDN'T I SAY THAT?

IF I DON'T THINK I'M GOING TO BE THE BEST,

WHY DO I PLAY?"

At one tournament in
Indian Wells, California,
in 2001, the audience booed her and
shouted racist insults at her throughout the
match. Even though she won the title, she cried in
the locker room and all the way home.

She refused to
play in that tournament for
another fourteen years.

Later that summer, Venus beat Serena in the final at the US Open. They had already been accused of MATCH FIXING during the tournament at Indian Wells, and were accused again, which was extremely serious. Sports players are supposed to give their best and compete fairly. It could be that these accusations came from racist people who couldn't believe that there could be two black tennis champions in one family. This was painful, confusing and unfair to Serena, and she felt unwelcome and afraid – but she didn't want it to hold her back.

MATCH FIXING: the illegal practice of pretending to play when the winner has already been decided.

"*I looked different.*

I SOUNDED DIFFERENT.

I dressed differently.

I SERVED DIFFERENTLY.

BUT WHEN I STEPPED ONTO

the court,

I COULD COMPETE WITH

ANYONE."

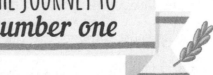

THE JOURNEY TO
number one

*I*n June 2002, Serena beat Venus at the French Open, her first Grand Slam win in three years. A few weeks later, on July 8, Serena faced Venus in the **Wimbledon final.** She knew it was now or never. She hadn't lost a set during the whole tournament, and she didn't lose one to Venus either. At championship point Serena's serve was huge, and Venus couldn't return it. **Serena had won** – beating the two-time Wimbledon champion!

She was presented with the winner's trophy by the president of the All England Lawn Tennis and Croquet Club, the Duke of Kent. She held it up, walking around the whole court showing it to the crowds. She couldn't stop grinning from ear to ear. At twenty years old she was the Wimbledon champion and the world's **number one** female tennis player.

From being three years old, standing on a potholed court in Compton, to holding the trophy of the oldest and most prestigious tennis competition in the world as the world's best female player ... it was just the beginning of the records that were to follow. Serena would have to face many ups and downs, but she was determined to *keep winning.* And in the process she made history over and over again.

There was only one thing better than being world number one, and that was holding *all four Grand Slam titles* at the same time! In 2002 and 2003 she succeeded in doing that. She faced Venus in the finals of all four, and she beat Venus each time.

Things get tough

Serena was riding high as the world's number one female tennis player. But despite this **well-deserved success** she faced a series of huge difficulties over the next few years.

Her parents Richard and Oracene had laid the foundations for her tennis training, working hard to coach her and support her as she grew up. In 2002 they got divorced. Even though Serena was an adult, she had to learn to accept the change.

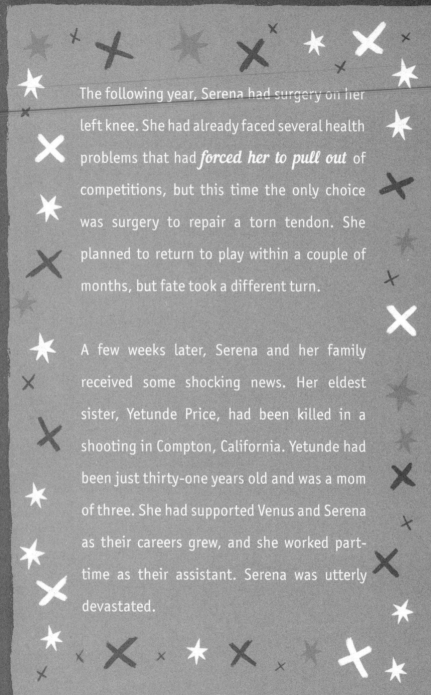

The following year, Serena had surgery on her left knee. She had already faced several health problems that had *forced her to pull out* of competitions, but this time the only choice was surgery to repair a torn tendon. She planned to return to play within a couple of months, but fate took a different turn.

A few weeks later, Serena and her family received some shocking news. Her eldest sister, Yetunde Price, had been killed in a shooting in Compton, California. Yetunde had been just thirty-one years old and was a mom of three. She had supported Venus and Serena as their careers grew, and she worked part-time as their assistant. Serena was utterly devastated.

In 2016 Serena and Venus opened a community center in Compton called the Yetunde Price Resource Center. Its aim is to enable people affected by violence to get the help they need.

The difficulties Serena was facing started to affect her focus on her tennis. She struggled over the next few years to keep her position at the top. In 2006 she fell out of the top 100. However, in the coming months and years, Serena would show the true mark of a champion in dealing with personal difficulties: RESILIENCE.

RESILIENCE: the ability to keep going when things get tough.

STRUGGLING
and winning

*A*t an all-time low, Serena started traveling to Africa. The trips helped Serena to connect with the roots that many black Americans have in Africa, where their ancestors lived before they were taken as slaves to America.

"*My dad always said*
YOU HAVE TO KNOW
YOUR HISTORY,
AND IF YOU KNOW
YOUR PAST,
YOU CAN HAVE A
great future."

Serena's charity work included **building a school** in Kenya and she was even involved in its construction.

"SEEING
WHERE SHE CAME FROM,
HOW WE GOT TO WHERE
WE ARE NOW,
SEEING THE PORTS WHERE
they shipped us off
AND THE LIFE OF OUR PEOPLE,
THAT REALLY CHANGED HER
ATTITUDE ABOUT BEING
a black woman."

– Oracene Price, Serena's mother

When she returned she was once again able to focus on her life and her career. She knew that she was returning to tennis for herself and no one else – because she wanted to play. Serena decided that if she was going to play tennis, she was going to win. Nobody believed she could do it. Some experts even said she had reached the end. But she didn't listen to any of the negativity. She also found meaning in her faith as a Jehovah's Witness. Her beliefs helped her manage a difficult emotional time and gave her *direction and strength*.

In 2007 she won a championship that everyone expected her to lose – the Australian Open in Melbourne. She *dedicated the win* to her sister Yetunde. She carried on believing in herself, and by 2008 she was world number one again, and she was better than ever before.

Frustrations running high

It was September 2009, and Serena was serving in the **semifinals** of the US Open. It was a crucial point in the match, as her opponent was only **two points** away from victory over Serena. As she threw the ball into the air the line judge called "fault!" causing her to lose the point. Now Serena was just one point away from **losing the match.**

Serena believed that the "fault" call was wrong and she was furious. Stressed and emotional, she started shouting at the line judge. The referee was called, and a point was given to her opponent. As a result, Serena lost the match. She was later punished for inappropriate behavior with fines totaling $82,500.

After the event Serena apologized. She said she handled the situation poorly, being overcome with passion and emotion. She has said that she is always working on managing her temper.

"I WILL LEARN *and grow* FROM THIS, AND BE A *better person* AS A RESULT."

Outbursts in tennis

There are strict rules about behavior on the court, and players can be punished if they break the rules. Often judges use their DISCRETION to overlook issues like foot faults if it is at a crucial moment because it can disrupt players and also upset audiences.

Tennis players are well known for angry outbursts. One of the most famous came from champion John McEnroe in 1981 who disagreed with the judge's call and shouted, "You cannot be serious!"

JOHN MCENROE 1981

DISCRETION: the freedom to decide what to do in any particular situation.

It is much more common for men to have outbursts when they play tennis — but they are often overlooked. Researchers say that women and black players are much more likely to be punished. This could be because it is still thought of as unladylike for women to get angry or emotional in public.

Research has also shown that even mild objection from black people can be interpreted as **high anger**. So though Serena knew she shouldn't have acted in anger, it's possible that the punishment she was given might be linked to the way women and black people are treated. It was something she would face again in her career. She always held her head with **pride**, and even though she suffered she used the chance to help people for the greater good. She played an important role as an **activist** and a champion for justice.

"WHY IS IT THAT WHEN *women get passionate,* THEY'RE LABELED EMOTIONAL, CRAZY, AND IRRATIONAL, BUT WHEN MEN DO THEY'RE *seen as passionate* AND STRONG?"

In 2018 Serena lost her temper again in a championship final against Naomi Osaka, and faced punishment. People wondered if she had only been punished because she was a black woman.

On that day in 2018 Serena also did something important: she congratulated Naomi Osaka for winning and apologized for spoiling a magical moment for the young champion. She was a gracious loser, and that's just as important as being an amazing winner.

More health problems

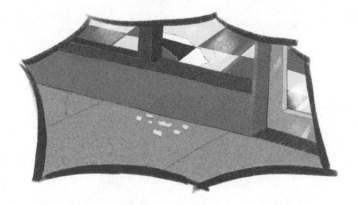

In the summer of 2010, while in a cafe in Germany, Serena stepped on some broken glass and needed surgery on her right foot. Then, in February 2011, a blood clot was found in her lung and she was given emergency treatment in the hospital. Again people wondered if she would be able to return to tennis, and again she **proved them wrong**. Just three months later, she was competing once more.

Also in 2011 her sister and best friend Venus was diagnosed with SJÖGREN'S SYNDROME. It affected her participation in tennis, but, just like Serena, Venus would also fight her setbacks and become a champion again.

SJÖGREN'S SYNDROME: an illness that attacks the immune system and causes joint aches and fatigue.

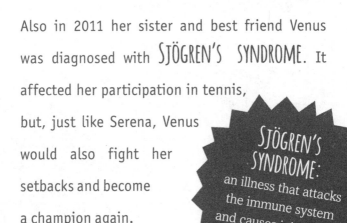

Growing as a person

Setbacks were now a familiar part of Serena's life, but she never listened to the people who doubted her. She knew that downs as well as ups are part of the journey of a champion, and the only person she should listen to was herself.

"I AM LUCKY
THAT WHATEVER
fear I have inside me,
MY DESIRE TO WIN
IS ALWAYS
stronger."

The health scares and her amazing comeback gave Serena a new attitude of joy in the sport that she loves so much:

"It's always good to have fun, ESPECIALLY AFTER EVERYTHING I'VE BEEN THROUGH. *It's all fun to me now.* THIS IS REALLY ALL A BONUS."

She had made her mark on tennis, and now she was ready to broaden what it meant to be Serena Williams. In the coming years she would break even more records, speak out against injustice and explore her many other talents.

The comeback queen

Over the next few years Serena started **breaking record after record.** In 2012 she became a double gold medalist at the Olympics in women's singles and doubles. This meant she held a "career golden slam" – all four Grand Slams and Olympic gold medals at the same time, only the fourth-ever person to do so.

At Wimbledon that year she served a tournament record of 102 ACES. The following year she served one of the top-three *fastest serves* ever by a woman.

ACE:
in tennis an ace is a serve that immediately wins the point.

Then Serena became number one again. At thirty-one she was the *oldest female tennis player* to make it to the top. She had been number one *six times* so far.

Serena had started fighting for women in tennis to be paid the same amount as men. Even though female tennis players trained just as hard and played as many competitions as men, their prize winnings were much less. Serena felt this was unfair. Along with other tennis players of both sexes she started campaigning for equality in the prizes. Eventually some of the big tournaments listened and made the prizes equal. So it was a cause for celebration when Serena won the biggest-ever prize in tennis of $4 million at the US Open in 2014!

Serena has spent time campaigning for **working women**, wherever they are, to have equal pay because it is still the norm that women are paid less for doing the same jobs as men. She also has been working hard to **fight racism** in tennis.

She was still affected by her experience at the Indian Wells tournament in 2001, but fourteen years later she wanted to show that things could change. She decided to play there again in 2015. Serena had to show something extraordinary in the face of her hurt and injustice: love and forgiveness.

At the tournament she supported a charity that helps people in need of a fair trial.

"TOGETHER WE HAVE A CHANCE TO WRITE *a different ending."*

Back on the tennis court Serena achieved another "Serena Slam." And in 2016 she added another record to her list: she came to the end of 186 weeks in the number one spot.

186 weeks is more than three and a half years!

Getting engaged

In 2015 Serena was in Rome to play in the Italian Open. One morning, she came down to eat breakfast at her hotel, and was waiting for her friends to join her at the next table. Instead, a tall man came and sat there. Serena felt annoyed – she had wanted to use that table!

The man's name was **Alexis Ohanian**. He was a very influential figure in the media and technology industry. Serena and her friends tried to get him to move. One of them even made up a story that there was a rat nearby, but he just replied, "I'm from Brooklyn. I see rats all the time."

Serena and Alexis started talking after that. By the end of the conversation he had agreed to come and watch her play that evening in the Italian Open. A few months later, he joined her in Paris for the French Open. They walked around the city for six hours and went to the zoo. Little did Serena know that this would be the man that she was going to marry. But before that she had a lot more tennis to play and many more challenges to overcome.

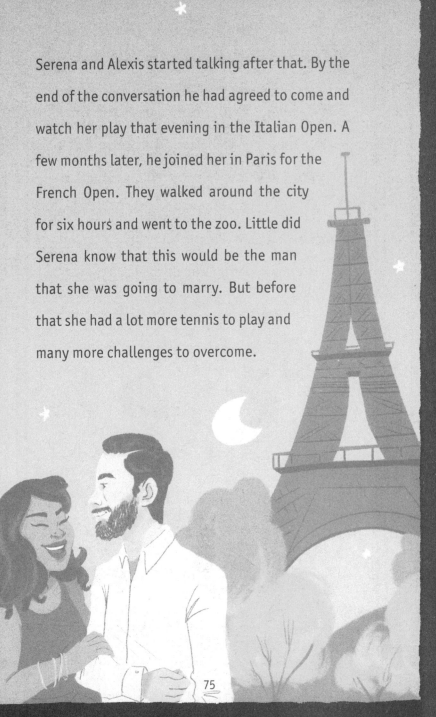

In December 2016, nearly a year and a half after they met in Rome, Alexis organized a *surprise trip* to the same hotel. He got on one knee and proposed to her. This time Alexis brought his own rat, although thankfully it was only made of plastic!

More records

*D*espite the excitement of getting engaged, Serena continued to focus on her training and her goal to **keep winning**. Her next big tournament was the Australian Open in January 2017. She worked hard – and won.

At the age of thirty-five she had extended her record as the oldest-ever number one. On top of that was another record: Serena's twenty-third Grand Slam title, the most titles won by a player in the open era.

Margaret Court holds the pre-open era record, with twenty-four titles.

MARGARET COURT 1942

Serena is always aiming bigger and higher; she is always pushing herself.

"IT'S NOT A SECRET THAT I HAVE *my sights on* TWENTY-FIVE."

Becoming a mom

There was one additional surprise that nobody apart from Serena, Alexis and a few close friends knew about Serena's **record-breaking win:** Serena had done all this while she was pregnant!

Later that year, on September 1, Alexis and Serena's daughter was born and they called her Alexis Olympia Ohanian Junior. Serena and Alexis were breaking CONVENTION by using this name – a first name that could be used for any gender, and using "Junior," which is often given to a boy. Serena wanted to show that girls have the same status as boys.

CONVENTION: tradition.

Serena was very ill after having the baby and needed emergency treatment. Even though she had planned to return to tennis within a few months, she had to make the difficult decision to wait until her body was ready.

For the first six weeks after the baby was born she couldn't get out of bed because she was so ill. Her husband looked after Alexis Olympia.

She spoke publicly about the various feelings of being a mom: happiness, guilt, tiredness and love, and how these **different emotions** can be difficult to manage. She said being a mom and working is hard, but she wanted to show that it could be done, and to talk publicly about it. By being honest Serena became a champion for moms too. She wanted to help others by being brave and talking about tough things from her own experiences.

Getting married

On November 16, 2017, Serena and Alexis got married at the Contemporary Arts Center in New Orleans. Baby Alexis Olympia was looked after by her aunt Venus.

The theme of the wedding was "Beauty and the Beast." The tables were named after each of Serena's Grand Slam wins. The party favors for guests to take home were in the shape of famous tennis trophies. Serena even had a pair of **bejeweled sneakers** for her special day. She said that she wanted to have a "strong" wedding.

"I FELT LIKE
a door had been opened
TO A PERSON WHO MADE ME
WANT TO BE MY BEST SELF.
I FIND MYSELF JUST WANTING TO BE BETTER
BY SIMPLY BEING
around her
BECAUSE OF THE
STANDARDS SHE HOLDS."

– Alexis Ohanian

Another return to tennis

Six months after Alexis Olympia was born, Serena played

her first match – and won!

When Serena went on maternity leave she was number one in the world, but when she returned fourteen months later she was number 451. That meant she was paid a lot less, just because she had a break to have a baby. Although Serena is fortunate enough to be wealthy, she used her voice to speak up for other women who were being paid less just for being a mom. She campaigned to change the rules for fair pay for mothers.

Going back to tennis after having a baby and health troubles was exciting but also difficult, and Serena was honest about the challenges. She still has lots of goals she wants to achieve! And Serena was true to her word: after becoming a mom she became the runner-up at Wimbledon in 2018.

"WHETHER STAY-AT-HOME

OR WORKING,

finding that balance with kids

is a true art.

YOU ARE THE TRUE HEROES.

I'M HERE TO SAY: IF YOU ARE HAVING

a rough day or week,

IT'S OK –
I AM TOO!"

A WOMAN WHO KEEPS
changing the world

*S*erena Williams has been playing professional tennis for nearly twenty-five years. She was number one at the age of twenty and again at thirty-five. She has already won twenty-three Grand Slam titles, more than any other tennis player – male or female – in the open era. Her record includes 308 Grand Slams and four Olympic gold medals. She has dominated the world of tennis for twenty years, and earned more prize money than any other female athlete in history – $88 million!

Ten of her Grand Slam wins came after turning thirty - including one while she was pregnant.

The GOAT

When it comes to tennis, some people believe Serena is the GOAT (**G**reatest **O**f **A**ll **T**ime). This includes existing tennis champions, so they should know!

John McEnroe says Serena is the "best female player ever."

Roger Federer says Serena isn't just the greatest female player of all time, but "overall," meaning of any gender.

Martina Navratilova agrees: "It's not just about how many slams you win or how many tournaments you win - it's just your game overall. And she's definitely got all the goods."

Serena's achievements have inspired many others too.

J. K. Rowling once said, "I love her. What an athlete, what a role model, what a woman!"

DID YOU KNOW?

Serena's favorite sport to watch other than tennis is gymnastics.

Fashion and self-expression

Serena always loved clothes and fashion. As a child she used to make clothes for her dolls. It was a skill she was serious about developing alongside her tennis career.

After she graduated from high school in 1999, she **enrolled to study fashion** at the Art Institute at Fort Lauderdale. In 2004 she launched her first clothing line, Aneres, which is "Serena" spelled backward.

Serena had also always enjoyed getting manicures. To launch her own nail collection she qualified as a nail technician. Some of her clients were celebrities like Oprah Winfrey. Then in 2015 she presented her own clothing collection at New York Fashion Week with the Home Shopping Network. In 2018 she launched her fashion label, Serena.

Using her body and clothes to express herself has always been important to Serena. She says what she wears on the court changes the way she plays. In 2019 she wore a superhero cape with the French words meaning "queen," "champion," "goddess," and "mom" to the French Open. Serena wanted to use her clothes to support moms like her, who were working hard for their families and their careers, and show that in their own way everyone can be champions and queens.

DID YOU KNOW?

In 2018, in the French Open, she wore a black catsuit that she said was inspired by the fictional country of Wakanda from the Marvel universe. She said it made her feel like a warrior. Her outfit was banned. So she came back the next day in a tutu.

In the 1880s men and women would dress up to play tennis. For women that meant dresses with boned corsets and huge skirts; for men that meant suits and ties.

Although English is Serena's native language, she also speaks French, Spanish and Italian. After matches in France she sometimes gives interviews in French.

Proud
of her body

Serena has appeared on the front of fashion, news and sports publications, proud of her style and her body, despite criticism she has received. She has always dressed how she wanted to on the court, although it hasn't always been allowed. Some people didn't like her being strong or athletic or having her own style.

"IF WE ALL
liked the same thing,
IT WOULD MAKE THE WORLD
A REALLY BORING PLACE!
WHAT MATTERS MOST IS
that I like myself."

She knew her body was a wonderful, powerful thing that had helped her to achieve her dreams. Despite many health challenges, each time her body was strong and **recovered**. It was her body that allowed her to be the greatest player that she could be, to become a fashion icon and to have a baby.

"THIS IS MY WEAPON and machine."

So much more

Serena is setting up a **cosmetics company** and owns a stake in the Miami Dolphins. Besides this, she is on the board of a technology company and runs a VENTURE CAPITAL company that invests money into new businesses run by people who have the biggest barriers to success – women, people of color and young entrepreneurs.

VENTURE CAPITAL COMPANY: a company that puts money into new businesses with the expectation that they will grow and they will get a share of the profits.

Venus and Serena purchased the stake in the Miami Dolphins together - the first African-American women to do so. Breaking records everywhere!

DID YOU KNOW?

She has a teacup Yorkie dog named Chip, which is short for Christopher Chip Rafael Nadal. She calls him her son.

Her own background and the challenges she has faced have made her realize that playing a charitable role is vital. She has worked with many charities, including the Yetunde Price Resource Center and the Serena Williams Foundation that she set up. Through these she helps people reach their goals by overcoming barriers, like education, gender, race or disability.

Her favorite author is Maya Angelou.

DID YOU KNOW?

She has helped both financially and with her own hands to build schools in Africa. She is also an International Goodwill Ambassador for UNICEF. She promotes education, an end to violence, and supports health charities that tackle diseases like cancer and HIV.

She is also a talented actor and has appeared on TV, in film and music. Some of the most famous things she has starred in are *The Simpsons*, *Pixels* and the Beyoncé visual album *Lemonade*. She even has her own TV series called *Being Serena*.

Serena writes books and newspaper articles, including biographies of her own life, and talks about issues that matter to her, like sexism, racism and motherhood.

Just the beginning

So what's next for Serena? She wants to win the most Grand Slams of any woman ever, and she continues to use her influence to make a difference in the world.

"What am I curious about now? HOW DO I WANT TO GROW NOW?"

Serena is changing the world simply by being who she is, which means always working hard to be the best. In fact, being different and standing out from the crowd is what has helped her. She didn't want to follow others, but instead be herself.

Sometimes she has made mistakes and sometimes she has faced difficulties, but through it all she has listened to her inner voice, even when people doubted her or said she was wrong. When she has lost she has been a gracious loser because she believes that there is space for everyone to succeed; she doesn't need to pull others down.

Instead, she believes that we should pull other people up with us.

DID YOU KNOW?

Tennis players traditionally shake hands at the beginning of a match and again at the end. The winner should congratulate the one who lost on having played a good match, and the one who lost should be well mannered in defeat.

When Serena sets her mind to something she's proved over and over that she can make it happen. Through her words and actions she has shown that a female champion isn't just a champion for women, but a champion for everyone.

"I DON'T THINK MY STORY is over yet."

September 26, 1981

Born in Saginaw, Michigan.
Family moves to Compton,
California, a few months
later.

1984

Serena starts
playing tennis at
the age of three.

1991

Achieves first place at the Junior
US Tennis Association Tour.
Venus and Serena start attending
the tennis academy of Rick Macci
in West Palm Beach, Florida.

October 1995
Turns professional.

1997
Reaches world
top-100 female
tennis players.

July 1998
First Grand Slam victory
in the mixed doubles at
Wimbledon.

1999
First singles Grand Slam victory at the US Open.
Reaches the world's top-ten female tennis players.
Enrolls at the Art Institute of Fort Lauderdale to
study fashion design.

September 2000

Wins a gold medal at the Olympics in women's doubles with Venus.

July 8, 2002

Becomes world number one at the age of twenty.

January 2003

Achieves career Grand Slam, which becomes known as the "Serena Slam."

August 1, 2003

Undergoes surgery to repair her left knee.

September 14, 2003

Older sister, Yetunde Price, is killed.

2008

Becomes number one again.
Establishes the Serena
Williams Foundation.

2009

Fined for bad behavior on the court.
Buys part of the Miami Dolphins
with Venus.

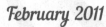

July 7, 2010

Requires surgery to
her right foot.

February 2011

Undergoes emergency treatment
for a blood clot in her lungs.

September 2011

Appointed UNICEF International Goodwill Ambassador.

2012

Serves a Wimbledon tournament record of 102 aces.
Double gold medalist at the Olympics in women's singles and doubles.

January 2013

Serves the third-fastest serve of all time among female players at 128.6 mph.

February 18, 2013

Becomes the oldest female tennis player to be number one at thirty-one (her sixth time at the top).

September 2014

Receives the biggest winnings payout ever in tennis history of $4 million at the US Open.

2015

Achieves a second "Serena Slam."

September 12, 2016

Serena's run of 186 weeks at number one finally comes to an end. This ties for the most consecutive weeks at number one.

December 29, 2016

Gets engaged to Alexis Ohanian.

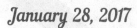

January 28, 2017

World number one again! Wins her twenty-third Grand Slam title to become the women's record holder in the open era. She was pregnant at the time.

September 1, 2017

Gives birth to Alexis Olympia Ohanian Jr. Spends a week in the hospital after clots affect her lungs and nearly dies.

November 16, 2017

Marries Alexis Ohanian.

May 2018

Launches her fashion label, Serena.

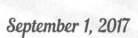

July 2018

Just ten months after having a baby and nearly dying from medical complications, Serena is a finalist at Wimbledon.

September 2018

Fined for inappropriate behavior against Naomi Osaka at the US Open.

2019

Reaches the singles final at Wimbledon, and the semifinals of the US Open.

SOME THINGS
to think about

*I*n Serena's journey there have been lots of ups and downs, including defeats. She says that the way you deal with defeat and even failure says more about you than how you win. What kind of challenges do you face, and what things can you do to overcome them?

Her husband says she is the most hard-working person he has ever met. Can you think of someone you respect who works really hard?

A big part of playing tennis is having a body that is strong, athletic and healthy. How do you feel about your body, and how does it help you do the things you want to do?

Can you think of any other champions that you admire? What has helped them become champions? You can research more about champions in different areas like science, literature, politics, film, sports or anything else you can think of. Maybe it will give you some ideas of a goal you want to set yourself!

If you were Serena Williams,
what would you do next?

More about tennis

WHO CAN PLAY TENNIS?

Everyone! But it wasn't always like that. Even though the first Wimbledon tournament was played in 1877, women had to protest until 1884 to be allowed to play.

PRIZE MONEY FOR MEN AND WOMEN

Serena Williams won the biggest-ever prize in tennis of $4 million. But on the whole men's prize money is much higher than what women receive. However, due to people's hard work and campaigning, this is changing.

COULD YOU BEAT SERENA WILLIAMS?

A study showed that twelve in one hundred men think that they could win a point from Serena Williams at tennis, but only three in one hundred women think so. Some people say that the reason men think they have a chance against her is because they don't take women seriously and underestimate women's talents. What do you think? Do you think you could win a point from her?

WHO INVENTED TENNIS?

There are stories of the ancient Greeks and Egyptians playing games like tennis. But today's game traces back to some French monks in the eleventh or twelfth century. They played *jeu de paume*, which involved hitting a ball backward and forward with the palms of their hands – this is why its name means "game of the palm."

HOW TO BECOME A TENNIS CHAMPION

Players gain points by winning matches in eligible competitions, particularly the "Grand Slams," then a ranking is compiled from the points. More than a thousand people are ranked. As soon as you earn your living by winning matches you are considered a "tennis pro."

Early tennis courts were long narrow rooms and players could hit the ball off the walls. The net was 1.5 meters (4.92 feet) high on the sides but drooped to 91 centimeters (3 feet) in the middle, which is today's height. Some courts were square and the floors were made of paving slabs. In 1874 an hourglass design for the court was submitted, but we have today's rectangular court thanks to the Wimbledon championships.

There are four types of court: clay, grass, hard and carpet. The surface of the court affects how the ball bounces, and that means some playing styles work better than others. A true champion – like Serena Williams – can master all the surfaces.

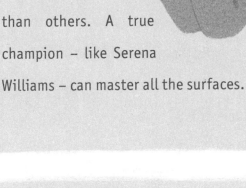

Tennis balls

The first balls that the monks played with were made of hair, wool or cork wrapped in string and cloth or leather. Some were even made of animal stomachs and others of putty (a type of paste) and human hair! Later they were stitched in felt and looked like a baseball. It was only in the 1850s, when rubber was invented, that the bouncy balls we use today were created. With more boingy balls the game could be played on grass, and that meant that tennis could move outdoors at last.

In 1972 tennis balls got their familiar fluorescent color, which is called "optic yellow." This allows the balls to be seen more easily by people watching television, rather than the white, gray or other colors often used.

Quote Sources

Direct quotes throughout are from the following sources:

Pages 5, 18: "6 Inspiring Lessons from Serena Williams" (*Forbes* online, 30 August 2019)

Page 6: http://www.tennisquotes.com/serena-williams.php

Page 15: "Serena Williams' Letter to the Dreamers," Porter Magazine's *Incredible Women of 2016*

Page 17: Serena Williams Facebook page (19 February 2016)

Page 20: "Venus and Serena Williams' childhood coach has an amazing story about realizing they could dominate first time he met them" (Scott Davis, *Business Insider*, 26 January 2017)

Page 25: "Who's Your Daddy?" (S. L. Price, *Vault*, 31 May 1999)

Page 32: "The fall and rise of maturing Serena Williams" (Ahmed Rizvi, *The National*, 10 September 2012)

Page 34: "Ignore the tabloids: Venus Williams just taught us the true meaning of sisterhood" (Kayleigh Dray, *Stylist*, 2019)

Page 36: "Serena Williams beats big sister Venus to set Grand Slam record" (BBC Newsround, 28 January 2017)

Page 40 "Serena Williams Exclusive Interview" (*Seventeen*, 1 Sep 2009)

Pages 41, 53: "Serena Williams sits down with Common to talk about race and identity" (*The Undefeated*, 19 December 2016)

Pages 44, 67, 73: "Serena Williams: I'm Going Back to Indian Wells" (Serena Williams, *Time*, 4 February 2015)

Page 55: "Road to 23: The story of Serena's path to greatness" (Alyssa Roenigk, *The Undefeated*, 8 September 2016)

Page 59: "Serena Williams Apologizes Before Winning Doubles Title" (David Waldstein, *New York Times*, 14 September 2009)

Pages 62, 96: "Serena Williams Poses Unretouched" (Serena Williams, *Harper's BAZAAR*, 9 July 2019)

Page 68: "Another winning return by Serena the comeback queen" (Paul Newman, *Independent*, 15 June 2011)

Page 78: "Serena Williams on Motherhood, Marriage, and Making Her Comeback" (Rob Haskell, *Vogue*, 10 January 2018)

Page 83, 103: "Serena Williams's Love Match" (Buzz Bissinger, *Vanity Fair*, 27 July 2017)

Page 86: @SerenaWilliams Instagram post (6 August 2018)

Page 95: "Serena Williams: "Not everyone's going to like the way I look" (Paula Cocozza, *Guardian*, 28 June 2016)

Have you read about all of these extraordinary people?

THE EXTRAORDINARY LIFE OF
NEIL ARMSTRONG

THE EXTRAORDINARY LIFE OF
ANNE FRANK

THE EXTRAORDINARY LIFE OF
STEPHEN HAWKING

THE EXTRAORDINARY LIFE OF
KATHERINE JOHNSON

THE EXTRAORDINARY LIFE OF
ROSA PARKS

THE EXTRAORDINARY LIFE OF
MALALA YOUSAFZAI

THE EXTRAORDINARY LIFE OF
AMELIA EARHART

THE EXTRAORDINARY LIFE OF
MAHATMA GANDHI

THE EXTRAORDINARY LIFE OF
MARY SEACOLE

THE EXTRAORDINARY LIFE OF
NELSON MANDELA

THE EXTRAORDINARY LIFE OF
SERENA WILLIAMS

THE EXTRAORDINARY LIFE OF
STEVE JOBS